W9-BGQ-079

AIR FORCE

SPECIAL FORCES: PROTECTING, BUILDING, TEACHING, AND FIGHTING

AIR FORCE

by Gabrielle Vanderhoof

Mason Crest

MASON CREST
370 Reed Road
Broomall, Pennsylvania 19008
www.masoncrest.com

Second Printing
9 8 7 6 5 4 3 2

Library of Congress Cataloging-in-Publication Data
Vanderhoof, Gabrielle.
  Air Force / by Gabrielle Vanderhoof.
      p. cm. — (Special forces)
  Includes bibliographical references and index.
  ISBN 978-1-4222-1837-2   ISBN (series) 978-1-4222-1836-5
  1. United States. Air Force—Commando troops—Juvenile literature. 2. Special forces (Military science)—United States—Juvenile literature. I. Title.
  UG633.V36 2011
  358.4—dc22
                                2010019186

Produced by Harding House Publishing Service, Inc.
www.hardinghousepages.com
Interior design by MK Bassett-Harvey.
Cover design by Torque Advertising + Design.
Printed in USA by Bang Printing.

With thanks and appreciation to the U.S. Military for the use of information, text, and images.

Contents

Introduction

Elite forces are the tip of Freedom's spear. These small, special units are universally the first to engage, whether on reconnaissance missions into denied territory for larger conventional forces or in direct action, surgical operations, preemptive strikes, retaliatory action, and hostage rescues. They lead the way in today's war on terrorism, the war on drugs, the war on transnational unrest, and in humanitarian operations as well as nation building. When large-scale warfare erupts, they offer theater commanders a wide variety of unique, unconventional options.

Most such units are regionally oriented, acclimated to the culture and conversant in the languages of the areas where they operate. Since they deploy to those areas regularly, often for combined training exercises with indigenous forces, these elite units also serve as peacetime "global scouts," and "diplomacy multipliers," beacons of hope for the democratic aspirations of oppressed peoples all over the globe.

Elite forces are truly "quiet professionals": their actions speak louder than words. They are self-motivated, self-confidant, versatile, seasoned, mature individuals who rely on teamwork more than daring-do. Unfortunately, theirs is dangerous work. Since the 1980 attempt to rescue hostages from the U.S. embassy in Tehran, American special operations forces have suffered casualties in real-world operations at close to fifteen times the rate of U.S. conventional forces. By the very nature of the challenges that face special operations forces, training for these elite units has proven even more hazardous.

Thus it's with special pride that I join you in saluting the brave men who volunteer to serve in and support these magnificent units and who face such difficult challenges ahead.

—Colonel John T. Carney, Jr., USAF–Ret.
President, Special Operations Warrior Foundation

U. S. AIR FORCE

VALOR

Saving the lives of your fellow Airmen is the most extraordinary kind of heroism that I know.

GENERAL CURTIS E. LEMAY
Fifth Chief of Staff, United States Air Force

When I think of the Enlisted Force I see Dedication, Determination, Loyalty and Valor.

CHIEF MASTER SERGEANT OF AIR FORCE PAUL W. AIREY
First Chief Master Sergeant of the United States Air Force

As I prepare for his...mission, I am a bit homesick... Mother and Dad, you are very close to me, and I long to so to talk to you. America has asked much of our generation, but I'm glad to give her all I have because she has given me so much.

SERGEANT ARNOLD RAHE
U.S. Army Air Forces, WWII, Killed In Action over France from a letter to his parents

COURAGE

Courage is rightly esteemed the first of human qualities... because it is the quality which guarantees all others.

SIR WINSTON CHURCHILL
Prime Minister of the United Kingdom during WWII

Courage is doing what you are afraid to do...

CAPTAIN EDWARD V. 'EDDIE' RICKENBACKER
Leading American Ace of WWI

It isn't just my brother's country, or my husband's country, it's my country as well. And so the war wasn't just their war it was my war and I needed to serve in it.

BEATRICE HOOD STROUP
Major, Woman's Army Corps, WWII

Our nation is blessed by the courageous families who give us our courageous Airmen.

GENERAL DAVID C. JONES
Ninth Chief of Staff, United States Air Force &
Ninth Chairman, Joint Chiefs of Staff

SACRIFICE

They knew not the day or hour nor the manner of their passing when far from home they were called to join that great band of heroic airmen that went before.

INSCRIPTION FROM THE AMERICAN CEMETERY AND MEMORIAL
Cambridge, England

...am going on a raid this afternoon...there is a possibility I won't return...do not worry about me as everyone has to leave this earth one way or another, and this is the way I have selected. If after this terrible war is over, the world emerges a saner place... pogroms and persecutions halted, then, I'm glad I gave my efforts with thousands of others for such a cause.

SERGEANT CARL GOLDMAN
U.S. Army Air Forces, WWII, B-17 Gunner, Killed In Action over Western Europe... from a letter to his parents

...tell them that we gave our todays for their tomorrows.

INSCRIPTION FROM THE ALLIED CEMETERY
North Assam, India

...Our military families serve right alongside those of us in uniform. A special thank you to all the spouses and children and moms and dads out there praying for your loved ones in harm's way —

CHAPTER 1

Overview of the Air Force

The United States Air Force is one of several branches of the U.S. Military, and it is also the youngest. Working alongside the Navy, Marine Corps, Army, and U.S. Coast Guard, the Air Force protects and defends the United States and its interests via air and space. To do this, the Air Force is responsible for all military satellites and operates a variety of aircrafts to defend the country and its missions. (The Air Force is supplemented by two other components, as well: the Air Force Reserves and the Air National Guard.)

HISTORY OF THE AIR FORCE

The branch of the military that we know today as the Air Force was not always organized in this way. In fact, the Air Force was not its own branch until after the end of World

War II, and from its birth, it has gone through a number of organizational changes to become what it is now.

The Air Force first operated under the Army and became the Aeronautical Division of their signal corps in 1907. Although the Wright brothers had flown the first airplane just a few years before, this division, with the help of brave and innovative soldiers, made rapid progress. The Wright brothers made the delivery of their first airplane in 1909, and after experimenting with a number of aircrafts, the First Aero Squadron, an operational unit, was officially formed in December 1913.

Nearly five years later, on July 18, 1914, the Army created the official Aviation section of the Signal Corps in hopes of expanding its flying capabilities. Just a few weeks later, though, the monumental landmark now known as World War I began in Europe. By the time the United States entered the war, Americans quickly realized that both their allies and enemies were far more advanced in terms of aircrafts and flight weapons. The United States tried to remain positive, but the rapidly advancing technology of Europe was simply too much for Americans to keep up with. President Woodrow Wilson knew that something had to be done.

The President acted quickly and created the Army Air Service on May 24, 1918, and by November of the same year, the Service had grown to include over 19,000 officers and 178,000 enlisted men. Although the Air Service was not quite up to speed in terms of weapons or plane development, it did succeed in bringing many well-trained pilots to Europe, where they flew mostly French-built planes. They became well known as a part of the American Expedition-ary Forces (AEF), and soon the United Kingdom created an independent air force, as well: the Royal Air Force, which became independent of the Royal Navy and British Army in April 1918.

The DH-4 was used by the U.S. Army Air Service both during and following World War I. Modeled from a combat-tested British De Havilland design, the DH-4 was the only U.S.-built aircraft to see combat during World War I.

Despite the United Kingdom's decision to create an air force separate from their other branches of military, the United States were not so quick to follow suit. Instead, the Army Reorganization Act of 1920 organized the force into yet another segment of the Army; the Air Force became an official combat arm of the branch, and soon after, the Air Corps Act of 1926 changed its name again to the Air Corps.

The real development of the Air Force began with the beginning of World War II in September 1939, when Adolf Hitler invaded Poland. As the war continued, the Axis powers—Germany, Italy, and Japan—continued to improve their armed forces, but the U.S. Air Force remained seemingly stagnant, with little financial input or growth. On June 20, 1941, two years after the war began, the U.S. Department of War created the Army Air Forces (AAF) to be its official aviation segment, and it soon became officially equal to the Army Ground Forces. The Air Corps was still a separate entity and acted as a combat arm of the Army.

By the end of the war, in 1944 and 1945, the American Air Forces had done a complete turn-around from their position at the beginning of the Second World War. In terms of aircraft development and achievements, the United States had all but defeated Germany and Japan. It would not be accurate to say that these powers were

UNDERSTAND THE FULL MEANING

Demobilization is the process of changing the function of something from a war basis to a peace basis, including disbanding troops.

Joint forces are any two or more military departments that operate under a single commander.

defeated thanks to air power alone, but it did help to seal the enemies' defeat.

As a result of the United States' complete demobilization of its armed forces after the war, just as after the First World War, the Air Force officially became independent of the Navy and Army on September 18, 1947. Stuart Symington was appointed the branch's first Secretary.

The importance and expansion of the Air Force continued with the emergence of the Cold War. The threats of communism against the United States quickly convinced American leaders that military forces needed to be stronger. The Soviet blockade of Berlin in 1948 created a new role for the U.S. Air Force, and showed just how vital the branch was to achieve American victory. In addition, the arms race pushed the Air Force into space with orbital satellites and other launch vehicles.

MISSION

The official mission of the United States Air Force is to *"fly, fight and win . . . in air, space and cyberspace."* According to the U.S. Air Force website, it has three distinct capabilities: developing Airmen, creating technology for war, and fighting and integrating operations. These capabilities and training entail the Air Force's six major skills.

AIR AND SPACE SUPERIORITY

With air and space superiority, joint forces can dominate enemy operations in all dimensions: land, sea, air, and space.

GLOBAL ATTACK

Because of technological advances, the Air Force can attack anywhere, anytime, and do so quickly and with great **precision**.

RAPID GLOBAL MOBILITY

This means being able to respond quickly and decisively anywhere they're needed.

PRECISION ENGAGEMENT

The ability to apply selective force against specific targets because of the nature and variety of future contingencies demands both precise and reliable use of military power with minimal risk and collateral damage.

INFORMATION SUPERIORITY

The ability of joint-force commanders to keep pace with information and incorporate it into a campaign plan is crucial.

AGILE COMBAT SUPPORT

Deployment and **sustainment** are keys to successful operations and cannot be separated. Agile combat support

UNDERSTAND THE FULL MEANING

Precision means accurate and exact.

The **deployment** of troops or weapons is to bring them into action on the field.

To **sustain** something is to maintain it; to keep something going.

An **expeditionary force** is a force organized to accomplish a specific goal or mission in a foreign country.

applies to all forces, from those permanently based to contingency buildups to **expeditionary forces**.

CORE VALUES

The Air Force has three core values that it teaches every Airman to live by: integrity first, service before self, and excellence in all they do. These values teach and challenge all airmen to always give their best in everything they do.

Airmen download C-17 Globemaster IIIs from five different Air Force bases on the ramp at Toussaint L'Ouverture International Airport Jan. 20, 2010, in Port-au-Prince, Haiti. Airmen delivered aid and rescue teams in the aftermath of a 7.0 magnitude earthquake that devastated Haiti.

INTEGRITY FIRST

Integrity is a character trait. It is the willingness to do what is right even when no one is looking. It is the moral compass, the inner voice, the voice of self-control, and the basis for the trust imperative in today's military.

Integrity is the ability to hold together and properly regulate all the elements of a personality. A person of integrity, for example, is capable of acting on conviction. A person of integrity can control impulses and appetites. But integrity also covers several other moral traits indispensable to national service: courage, honesty, responsibility, **accountability**, justice, openness, self-respect, and humility.

SERVICE BEFORE SELF

An airman's professional duties always take **precedence** over personal desires. At the very least, this includes the following behaviors:

- *Rule following:* To serve is to do one's duty, and our duties are most commonly expressed through rules. While it may be the case that professionals are expected to exercise judgment in the performance of their duties, good professionals understand that rules have a reason for being—and the default position

UNDERSTAND THE FULL MEANING

To be **accountable** for something is to be responsible for it; to answer to your actions.

To take **precedence** over something is to come before it; to have more importance.

Airmen Greg Graham, Brett Huette and Branden Hartlove, security forces trainees with the 343rd Training Squadron at Lackland Air Force Base, Texas, take measurements while framing a Habitat for Humanity house Feb. 6, 2010. The Airmen are taking part in the 343rd TRS SHIELD—Service, Honor, Integrity, Excellence and Leadership Development—program, which emphasizes character building.

must be to follow those rules unless there is a clear, operational reason for refusing to do so.

- *Respect for others:* Service before self tells us also that a good leader places the troops ahead of his or her

These soldiers are Special Operations Command's combat controllers. Their mission is to deploy undetected into combat and hostile environments to establish assault zones or airfields, while simultaneously conducting air traffic control, fire support, command and control, direct action, counter-terrorism, foreign internal defense, humanitarian assistance and special reconnaissance in the joint arena.

personal comfort. We must always act in the certain knowledge that all persons possess fundamental worth as human beings.

EXCELLENCE IN ALL WE DO

Excellence in all we do directs us to develop a sustained passion for continuous improvement and innovation that will propel the Air Force into a long-term, upward spiral of accomplishment and performance.

PRODUCT/SERVICE EXCELLENCE

We must focus on providing services and generating products that fully respond to customer wants and anticipate customer needs, and we must do so within the boundaries established by the tax-paying public.

PERSONAL EXCELLENCE

Military professionals must seek out and complete professional military education, stay in physical and mental shape, and continue to refresh their general educational backgrounds.

COMMUNITY EXCELLENCE

Community excellence is achieved when the members of an organization can work together to successfully reach a common goal in an atmosphere that is free from fear and that preserves individual self-worth. Some of the factors influencing interpersonal excellence are:

- *Mutual respect:* viewing another person as an individual of fundamental worth. Obviously, this means that a person is never judged on the basis of an attribute having to do with racial, ethnic, economic level, or gender.

- *Benefit of the doubt:* an attitude that says all coworkers are innocent until proven guilty. Before rushing to judgment about a person's behavior, it is important to have the whole story.

RESOURCES EXCELLENCE

Excellence in all we do also demands that we aggressively implement policies to ensure the best possible management of resources. Military professionals have an obligation to ensure that all of the equipment and property they ask for is mission essential. This means that residual funds at the end of the year should not be used to purchase "nice-to-have" add-ons. Human resources excellence means that we recruit, train, promote and retain those who can do the best job for us.

OPERATIONS EXCELLENCE

There are two kinds of operations excellence: internal and external. Internal excellence pertains to the way we do business internal to the Air Force from the unit level to Air Force Headquarters. It involves respect on the unit level and a total commitment to maximizing the Air Force team effort. Excellence of external operations pertains to the way in which we treat the world around us as we conduct our operations. In peacetime, for example, we must be sensitive to the rules governing environmental pollution, and in wartime we are required to obey the laws of war.

Airman's Creed

The Airman's promise to country and colleagues:

I am an American Airman.

I am a warrior.

I have answered my nation's call.

I am an American Airman.

My mission is to fly, fight, and win.

I am faithful to a proud heritage,

A tradition of honor,

And a legacy of valor.

I am an American Airman,

Guardian of freedom and justice,

My nation's sword and shield,

Its sentry and avenger.

I defend my country with my life.

I am an American Airman:

Wingman, leader, warrior.

I will never leave an airman behind.

I will never falter,

And I will not fail.

CHAPTER 2
Air Force Special Forces

"To protect the United States via air and space": this is the basic goal of the U.S. Air Forces, and why soldiers join the Force—to protect their country, its people, and its interests. Within the branch, though, there are several smaller and more specialized branches, known as Special Forces, or "special tactics." Each of these tactics is more physical, more extreme, and just as honorable and important a job as any in the military. These Special Forces include Combat Control, Pararescue, Special Operations Weather, and Tactical Air Control, and require as much, if not more specialized physical and intellectual training than a job in the general Air Force would.

COMBAT CONTROL

Combat controllers are some of the most highly trained personnel in any branch of the U.S. military. They must be certified Federal Aviation Administration air traffic controllers, and undergo a 35-week training course learning a number of unique skills.   The mission of an Air Force combat controller is a complex one: to go into combat, undetected, and establish assault zones or **airfield**s, while also conducting air traffic control, **fire support**, **command and control**, **direct action**, counter-terrorism, foreign internal defense, humanitarian assistance, and special **reconnaissance** in the area. In other words, they are committed to leading the way and making sure the path is safe for other troops to follow. The Combat Control motto is "First There," and demonstrates their commitment to the most dangerous mis-

UNDERSTAND THE FULL MEANING

An **airfield** is a landing and take-off area for aircrafts.

Fire support is long-range firepower (force from weaponry) provided to a front-line military unit. Typically, fire support is provided by artillery or close-air support.

Command and control is the exercise of authority and direction by a commander over assigned and attached forces in the accomplishment of the mission; also called C2.

Direct action is the strategic use of immediately effective acts, such as strikes, demonstrations, or sabotage, to achieve a political or social outcome.

Reconnaissance is the process of obtaining information about the position, activities, and resources of an enemy.

An **airdrop** is a delivery of supplies or troops by parachute from an aircraft.

Fundamentals are the basic principles of a subject; the building blocks for more complex training or information.

sions behind enemy lines. In addition, combat controllers are often called upon to assist in international emergences and humanitarian relief efforts, such as the recent 2010 tragic earthquake in Haiti.

HISTORY

Combat controllers originated in 1943 as Army pathfinders, out of a need for accurate **airdrops** during airborne campaigns of World War II. These pathfinders led the main troops into dangerous areas to provide weather information and guidance in order to best protect the U.S. soldiers.

Once the Air Force became its own service separate from the army, the pathfinders became known as combat control teams and were activated in 1953 to provide navigational aids and air traffic control for the growing Air Force. They became even more useful in the Vietnam War when they helped ensure mission safety and expedited air-traffic control.

TRAINING

The thirty-five weeks of special training to become a combat controller is broken down into very specific groups to cover every skill these Special Operations soldiers will need. The course begins with a two-week orientation at Lackland Air Force Base in Texas, focusing on the **fundamentals** and the history of combat control. Over the next nine months, trainees are sent to eight different locations in the southeast and western United States to undergo intense training for everything from survival skills and parachuting to scuba diving, underwater mobility, and land navigation.

Pararescuemen primarily function as personnel recovery specialists, with emergency medical capabilities in humanitarian and combat environments. PJs participate in search and rescue, combat search and rescue, recovery support for NASA and conduct other operations as appropriate.

COMBAT DIVER COURSE

In Panama City, Florida, at the U.S. Air Force base, PJs learn to use SCUBA and closed-circuit diving equipment to become combat divers. They are trained for over six weeks, and learn

UNDERSTAND THE FULL MEANING

Covertly means secretly.

to **covertly** take over areas, conduct sub-surface searches, and perform basic recovery operations.

UNDERWATER EGRESS TRAINING

At the Naval Air Station in Pensacola, Florida, trainees are taught specific skills over just one day of instruction, learning how to safely escape from a water-crashed or sinking aircraft.

BASIC SURVIVAL SCHOOL

PJs spend two and a half weeks at the U.S. Air Force Base in Fairchild, Washington, learning basic survival techniques for remote areas. Training includes principles, procedures, equipment, techniques to survive in extreme climates and harsh environments, and how to return home safely.

A pararescueman prepares a raft for a survivor during a crash recovery scenario in the Gulf of Mexico. He is assigned to the 38th Rescue Squadron from Moody Air Force Base, Ga., and is taking part in the base's operational readiness exercise, Commando Angel.

FREE-FALL PARACHUTIST SCHOOL

This five-week course in Fort Bragg, North Carolina, and the Yuma Proving Grounds in Arizona teach **wind tunneling**, and in-air instruction on things such as **aerial** maneuvers, air sense, and parachute opening procedures.

PARAMEDIC COURSE

The longest course in a PJ's training, this EMT-paramedic certification lasts twenty-four weeks at Kirtland Air Force Base in New Mexico. Trainees learn field medical care and **extrication** basics, field tactics, **mountaineering**, combat tactics, advanced parachuting, helicopter insertion/extraction, and become qualified as pararescue recovery specialists for assignment to any pararescue unit worldwide.

SPECIAL OPERATIONS WEATHER

Special Operations Weathermen are Air Force meteorologists with training to operate in **hostile** or **denied territory**. They gather, assess, and interpret weather from deployed locations and work with Air Force and Army Special Operations Forces. They create mission-tailored forecasts and train joint force members to take and communicate limited weather observations. In addition, these weathermen conduct special reconnaissance, organize, establish, and maintain weather data reporting networks, determine **host nation** meteorological capabilities, and train foreign national forces. Every Special Operations mission is planned using the intelligence and coordination of special operations weathermen.

HISTORY

The Special Operations Weathermen originated as the U.S. Army Weather Service in 1917 to provide the American Expeditionary Forces with "all the meteorological information needed; and to undertake special investigations in military meteorology and related problems." They first took part in combat operations during World War I in France in 1918.

In 1947, the Weather Service became a part of the newly independent Air Force. Since its birth, the force has helped out in every U.S. war involvement. In World War II, members of the Weather Service were referred to as guerrilla weathermen; they provided weather intelligence in support of air strikes, airlifts, and airdrops. During the Vietnam War, special warfare weathermen provided observations and established weather networks in Cambodia and Laos.

UNDERSTAND THE FULL MEANING

Wind tunneling involves using a vertical wind tunnel, in which air is blown upward at high speeds, to train parachutists and skydivers.

Aerial means having to do with the air, or something that is done in the air.

To **extricate** something is to release it from an entanglement or difficulty; to disengage it.

Mountaineering is the climbing of mountains for sport and fitness, usually incorporating the skills of rock climbing and climbing on ice.

If something is **hostile** it is relating to, or characteristic of, an enemy.

A **denied territory** is a territory held by the enemy; hostile territory.

The **host nation** is the country accepting military aid from its allies.

On May 5, 2008, the Air Force approved the establishment of a new Air Force Specialty Code for Special Operations Weather, formally recognizing their commitment to deploy into restricted environments by air, land, or sea to conduct weather operations, observe, and analyze all weather data and environmental intelligence.

TRAINING

Like all other special operations troops, Special Operations weathermen are also some of the most highly trained personnel. They must have the same weather weapon system qualification as all Air Force weathermen, but they also have to be qualified in advanced special tactics skills. They have a rigorous sixty-one-week training block with eight distinct courses.

Trainees begin at the U.S. Army Airborne School in Fort Benning, Georgia, and also learn parachuting skills in a three-week course. They then spend various lengths of time—from a few days to a few months—learning land- and water-survival training. The last and longest part of qualification is a twelve- to fifteen-month program in Hurlburt Field, Florida, where they will go through three phases of training: initial skills, core tasks, and operational readiness. These three phases test the trainees both physically and mentally to turn them into special operations weathermen.

UNDERSTAND THE FULL MEANING

If something is **lethal** or is full of **lethality**, it is capable of causing death.

TACTICAL AIR CONTROL

The Tactical Air Control Party (TACP) is a very physically, mentally, and technically demanding job, and it's one of the few true front-line combat jobs in the Air Force. TACPs have plenty of combat experience, and they're rich in military tradition. These soldiers are highly sought after throughout the world for the overwhelming combat power and lethality they bring to the battlefield. They provide numerous critical functions on the modern battlefield including:

- advising ground forces on aircraft employment and capabilities.
- coordinating and controlling aerospace operations.
- participating in battle planning.

HISTORY

The history of the TACPs' forerunner, Close Air Support, or CAS, goes back to World War I in the Pyrenees Mountains, where these pilots earned great respect from ground troops. However, their progress took two steps back in World War II, when the focus was on high-altitude bombing, and CAS was only performed when nothing better could be done, or when the situation on the ground was critical.

After both Korea and Vietnam, Close Air Support was finally taken seriously with the development of the A-10, a type of fighter jet. The A-10 provided the army with amazing tank-killing power, which meant that Air Force fighter pilots on the ground came in handy. Soon, small Air Force detachments sprang up at each army division, which provided a local group of Local Air Force Air Liaison Officers, or ALOs. Eventually, the enlisted terminal attack controller, or ETAC, career field was created and new units called Tactical Air Control Parties (TACPs) were enlisted to ensure that there were enough fighter pilots. ETACs are assigned to TACPs in all types of units from Airborne, Air Assault, Armor, Ranger, and Special Forces.

TACP OPERATIONS

If your goal is to become a TACP officer, you will operate and maintain cutting-edge technology, including communications, computers, digital networks, targeting and surveillance equipment, and various special-purpose tactical vehicles. You will develop valuable combat-related skills such as map-reading, compass usage, enemy-target location, survival, escape and evasion techniques, small-unit tactics, camouflage techniques, and hostile environment operations, while at the same time mastering a variety of weapons.

TACPs advise the Army ground commander on the capabilities and limitations of Air, Space, and Cyber assets. TACPs are responsible for planning, coordinating, and controlling close-air support missions in the battle area. TACP missions will require you to observe the battle area, identify hostile targets, and pinpoint their locations using many types of equipment such as the global-positioning system (GPS), laser rangefinders, and laser target designators.

Members attend the U.S. Air Force Combat Survival School immediately following technical school. Other schools that you may be able to attend, depending on mission needs and availability, include Airborne, Air Assault, Pathfinder, Ranger, HALO (Military Free Fall), and Sniper. TACPs also receive training from multi-service training from multi-service representatives on a wide variety of weapons.

U.S. Air Force Berets

The wearing of berets in the Air Force began in the 1970s, starting with the black beret in 1979, which was authorized for wear by personnel in the Tactical Air Control Party. In 1984, two airmen from Pope Air Force Base, North Carolina, submitted a design for the flash and crest design, which was approved for wear in 1985. Air Liaison Officers are also authorized to wear the black beret after graduation from the Joint Firepoint Control Course at Nellis Air Force Base in Nevada. Instead of the crest, they wear their rank insignia on the beret. Air Mobility Liaison Officers are authorized to wear the black beret in the Air Force, as well.

In addition to the black berets worn by TACP, ALOs, and AMLOs, colored berets are also worn as follows:

- maroon—Pararescue
- red (scarlet)—Combat Controllers
- royal blue—Security Forces
- grey—Combat Weather

CHAPTER 3

Modern Campaigns

The United States Air Force and its special operations forces work hard, in every aspect, to protect the U.S., its people, its environment, and even those in other countries, outside of the United States. Each branch of the Special Forces has specific missions they work toward, whether these involve homeland security or a humanitarian project in a developing country. Although every airman has his own specialty in which he is trained, all airmen are there to support one another in times of trouble, and to work together toward a common goal.

HUMANITARIAN RELIEF

U.S. airmen work hard in conditions that are often unconventional, ones that can be tough on the mind and body. The spirit of a United States Air Force member is a giving one, with a desire to help those who do not have the means to help themselves. The training discussed in chapter two helps to prepare an airman for these missions and utilize the skills they learn to help others.

COMBAT CONTROL IN HAITI

On January 12, 2010, one of the worst earthquakes in recent history struck Port-au-Prince, Haiti. Killing and injuring thousands of people, the earthquake had already done much of

Combat controllers talk to aircraft circling the Toussaint L'Ouverture International Airport Jan. 23, 2010, in Port-au-Prince, Haiti. The Airmen are from the 23rd Special Tactics Squadron at Hurlburt Field, Fla. (U.S. Air Force photo/Staff Sgt. Desiree N. Palacios)

its damage within the first few minutes of occurring, but the aftermath only made things worse. At 1:30 in the morning on January 13, combat controllers from the 23rd Special Tactics Squadron responded to a call and almost immediately deployed to Haiti to respond to the tragedy.

On the island, the combat controllers' main job was to command air traffic control. The damage from the earthquake, along with an overly congested airport and skies, were putting people in even more danger. For two straight weeks, the squad worked to bring order to the Toussaint L'Ouverture International Airport and its air operations. Developing a rotation called the "Haitian Maneuver," the combat controllers safely and efficiently cleared the runway to make room for vehicles to take off and land.

PARARESCUERS IN HAITI

While taking control of the air operations in post-earthquake Haiti was extremely important, the more urgent mission was to assist in taking care of the thousands of injured Haitians. The critical care air transport team, or CCATT, worked alongside the 45th Aeromedical Evacuation Squadron to evacuate the most critically injured individuals from the ground and into medical centers in the United States. CCATTs are highly specialized, rapidly deployable medical teams that set up and provide life-sustaining portable intensive care aboard transport aircraft in flight. In other words, these individuals are trained not only to safely transport individuals with the most severe injuries, but also to assist them while in transport to a more permanent and capable medical facility.

In completing this mission, these pararescuers transported many people with crush injuries, burns, and head trauma, as well as amputees. The CCATTs are extremely good at what they do, and they quickly moved patients from Haiti to U.S. hospitals. Although working with people who have been through a natural disaster can be a difficult and painful job, it is ultimately rewarding. Captain Jeffrey Marsh, an intensive care unit nurse explains, "It's really hectic, really stressful, because of the situation in the country. You normally don't get this type of experience in a career, so I am very happy to be a part of it."

BATTLING VIRUSES IN THE PHILIPPINES

Not only does the U.S. Air Force come to the rescue in tragedies that are breaking news, but they also offer their help in situations that are ongoing.

The Philippines is a country that deals with thousands of deaths each year as a result of Dengue fever, a mosquito-borne virus that spreads rapidly in the country's climate. In February 2010, Major Stephen Wolf visited the country for a week to educate residents on what causes the disease, how it spreads, and how to combat it. Major Wolfe is one of only fifteen **entomologists** in the U.S. Air Force, and the information he brought the country is invaluable. In the week that he was there, Major Wolfe visited a total of seventeen villages and reached 465 citizens, educating them on how to prevent Dengue fever.

UNDERSTAND THE FULL MEANING

An **entomologist** is a scientist who studies insects.

Major Stephen Wolf picks up a Center for Disease Control-approved mosquito trap he set the previous day at the Lapaz village during Operation Pacific Angel February 16, 2010, in Laoag, Philippines. Major Wolf is an entomologist from Kadena Air Base, Japan. (U.S. Air Force Photo/Capt. Genieve David)

He brought Dengue prevention literature, provided demonstrations, and with the help of a translator, explained in detail how to go about storing water, which is one of the prime breeding grounds for mosquitoes. Now, the Philippine air force has begun building its own preventative medicine program, modeling it after that of the U.S. Operation Pacific Angel. Operation Pacific Angel is a humanitarian and civic assistance program aimed at improving military civic cooperation between the United States and countries throughout the Asia-Pacific region.

AID TO AFGHANISTAN

Since the United States is currently in a "war on terror," humanitarian aid is probably not the first thing that comes to your mind when you think of a country like Afghanistan. But in April 2010, members of the 455th Expeditionary Aerial Port Squadron transported more than 1,100 pounds of humanitarian aid to Bagram Airfield in Afghanistan.

The mission began when Brigadier General Steven L. Kwast, the commander of the 455th Air Expeditionary Wing, sent out a message that hospital personnel had noticed a lot of children coming in with no shoes. When Technical Sergeant Ronald Knight got word of the situation, he asked his family back home in the States to collect whatever shoes they did not use, and send them to Afghanistan. The project soon caught on, and shoes were sent to the country, which were then distributed throughout hospitals in Bagram and orphanages in surrounding cities.

U.S. military members donate supplies to Afghan residents during a recent Operation Care humanitarian aid mission April 5, 2010, outside of Bagram Airfield, Afghanistan. The Operation Care team donated clothing, shoes, and other items to residents in need. (U.S. Air Force photo/Staff Sgt. Richard Williams)

PROVIDING BACKUP SUPPORT IN TIME OF WAR

WEATHER EXPERTS ASSIST ARMY PILOTS

U.S. troops must often confront unexpected weather conditions, so backup assistance from weathermen not only makes their job easier but safer as well. A four-person team in the Tactical Operations Center, or TOC, provided this backup in Iraq. These airmen worked in the brigade's TOC and

JOINT BASE BALAD, Iraq—Tech Sgt. Mike Adcock, a Task Force 38 weather forecaster, monitors a dust storm in northern Iraq on a satellite-produced image. (U.S. Army photo by Staff Sgt. Jeff Lowry)

Staff Sgt. Jody Ball releases a weather balloon during a special operations' weather team exercise. Sergeant Ball is a weatherman with the 10th Combat Weather Squadron.

Two members of an Iraqi police department place posters on a community wall during a joint presence patrol April 4, 2010, near Rufush, Iraq. (U.S. Air Force photo/Master Sgt. Trish Bunting)

monitored the weather in order to keep army pilots and leaders on top of the weather conditions. The Task Force completed thirty-eight missions in transporting VIPs throughout Iraq during Operation Iraqi Freedom. Their special training and skills allow them to judge ceiling and visibility limits that are affected by things like dust and smoke, as well as read and operate the extremely complicated computer systems that assist them.

SECURITY FORCES HELP IRAQI POLICE

After many years of non-stop war and permanent battle zones in Iraq, the country, in some ways, is now beginning to get its feet back on the ground and maintain a more normal everyday life for its citizens. One of the main problems that comes with this, though, is the need for the Iraqi police force to be able to handle the normal demands of citizens. Because the police have been trained for so long to only react to attacks and violence, they do not know how to do much else for the people. That is where the 732nd Expeditionary Security Forces came in. These airmen have worked with the Iraqi police, and trained them on how to conduct basic patrolling and interact with villagers.

This interaction with citizens will build the foundation of a more positive and trustworthy relationship between Iraq officials and the people. The police will be seen in a more positive light, allowing the people to come to them with their problems, even disclose important information regarding crime. After the first patrol with the Airmen, there was already positive feedback. First Lieutenant Abidalla Hady said he really liked going out and interacting with the people: "At the same time, I like to do something for them. Not just talk to them, but also truly help them. I want to know what they are suffering from so we can do something. Because we have to help them and make things happen."

SPY PLANES GET NEW USES

According to top Air Force commander, General Stanley McChrystal, one of the military's newest top priorities in Afghanistan is improving the lives of citizens and limiting civilian casualties. Before, Air Force spy planes' sole focus was to track **insurgent**s; now, the goal is to monitor developments in the daily life of Afghans. Instead of gathering intelligence for attack purposes, General McChrystal wants to use this information to protect civilians. For example, finding out where the Taliban have set up bases will allow the Air Force to send troops where they are needed most—and avoid areas where civilians might be injured.

The need to protect civilian lives is becoming more and more of a priority as time goes on. Colonel Mark Cooter, commander of the 497th Intelligence, Surveillance, and Reconnaissance Group at Langley, Virginia, says that the new challenge for intelligence officers is finding the right way to measure success in Afghanistan. For example, monitoring lines at gas stations will help determine if there are local shortages, and noting whether people are active at night

UNDERSTAND THE FULL MEANING

An **insurgent** is another word for a rebel; someone who revolts against a government or civil authority.

Spy planes are seeing their role in Afghanistan expand beyond intelligence gathering. A Global Hawk is shown landing at Beale Air Force Base, California.

or holed up in their homes will help commanders determine whether or not there is insurgent activity in the area.

SPACE AND TECHNOLOGY

INNOVATIONS IN BIOFUEL

In addition to contributing to humanitarian and military efforts, the Air Force is recognized as the leading branch when it comes to new technology and space intelligence. As the rest of the world is slowly becoming more eco-friendly in recent years, the Air Force is doing its part by creating cleaner ways to fuel military aircrafts.

An A-10C Thunderbolt II from Eglin Air Force Base, Florida, flies along the coast of Florida March 25, 2010, during the first flight of an aircraft powered solely by a biomass-derived jet fuel blend. The A-10 was fueled with a 50/50 blend of Hydro treated Renewable Jet and JP-8. (U.S. Air Force photo/Senior Master Sgt. Joy Josephson)

On March 25, 2010, an A-10 Thunderbolt flew solely on a blend of biomass-derived fuel and conventional JP-8 jet fuel. It was the first flight of its kind. Jeff Braun, the Air Force Material Command Fuels expert; Tim Edwards, a senior chemical engineer in the Air Force Research Laboratory's propulsion directorate; and Betty Rodriguez, the chief engineer for the **alternative fuels** certification office, directed the research

UNDERSTAND THE FULL MEANING

Alternative fuels are any types of fuel other than gasoline or diesel that are used to power motor vehicles; they also have improved energy efficiency and cause less air pollution than traditional fuels.

that went into the development of these "green" fuels. The A-10 was powered by a combination of conventional fuel and a biomass fuel derived from camelina, a nonfood rotation crop similar to soybean and mustard. This was part of a new family called HRJ fuels, or "hydro-treatable renewable jet" fuels.

The purpose of these jet fuels is to increase mile-per-gallon efficiency while decreasing the Force's carbon footprint—and at the same time, not sacrificing the high-performance standards to which the Air Force holds itself. Ms. Rodriguez explained that the Air Force is "at the cutting edge of alternative fuels." Currently, the Air Force is the U.S. Defense Department's largest consumer of jet fuel, but burns only the equivalent of a mid-sized airline. Force specialists are now working with natural things such as algae and other plant oils to create a more permanent source of fuel for the future to continue working toward keeping the planet "green."

AIRCRAFT RADARS

Airmen are often called on to solve even the most out-of-the-box problems that may arise—issues to which only highly trained soldiers can develop solutions. One of these solutions is the bird-detection radar stationed at Bagram Airfield in Afghanistan.

Over the past several years, observers noted that the base in Bagram had the highest bird-strike incident statistics of all the Air Force's bases in the Middle East. It happened that this base was located directly in the path of migratory birds

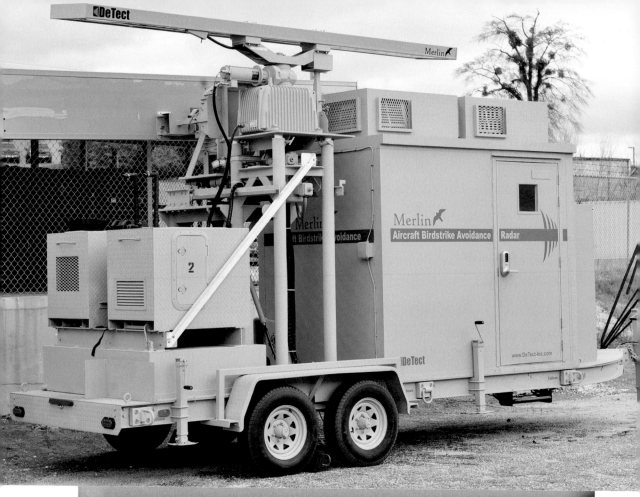

A Merlin Aircraft Birdstrike Avoidance Radar System is shown at Shaw Air Force Base, S.C. The MABARS is being delivered to Bagram Airfield, Afghanistan. (Courtesy photo)

in the spring—and since the base supports a combat zone, it was nearly impossible to completely shut down flights when bird "traffic" was at its peak. When these birds, especially in large flocks, collided with or flew into the engines of aircrafts, it not only was very bad for the birds, but it endangered the safety of the people on board and made it difficult for the pilot to make a safe emergency landing. Even if a safe landing were possible, the engines, more often than not, suffered millions of dollars of damage. In the worst possible scenario, the birds could even cause an airplane crash.

As a way to decrease the number of these incidents, the Safety Center's Bird Aircraft Strike Hazard (BASH) team at Kirkland Air Force Base, New Mexico, and the U.S. Air Force's Central Command Safety Office at Shaw Air Force Base collaborated to create bird-detection radar. This allowed officials to see the birds both day and night, with greater viewing-power than high-powered binoculars; the new technology also allowed pilots to be warned if they were flying into dangerous territory, helping them to avoid a situation before it was too late.

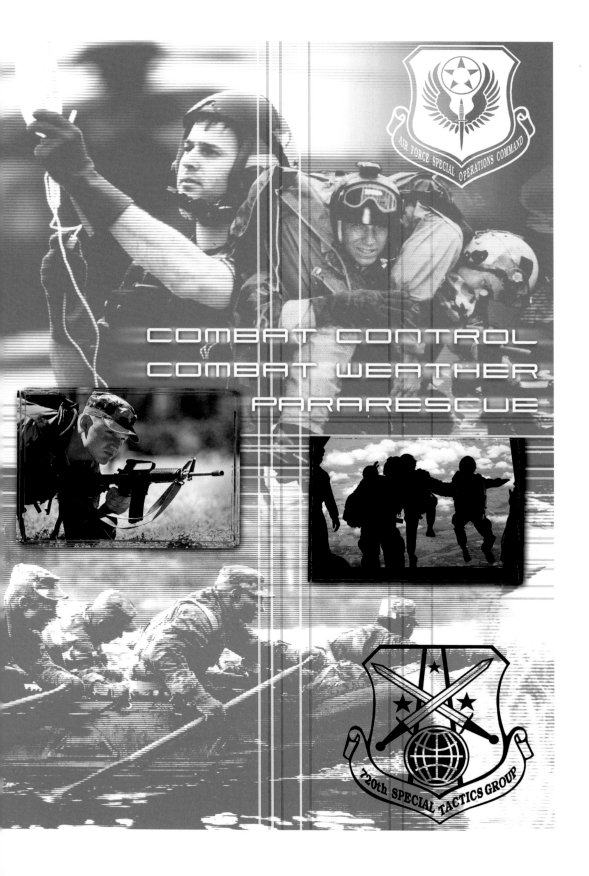

COMBAT CONTROL
COMBAT WEATHER
PARARESCUE

AIR FORCE SPECIAL OPERATIONS COMMAND

720th SPECIAL TACTICS GROUP

CHAPTER 4
Special Tactics Selection

Members of the Air Force Special Operations Command have some of the most extreme job descriptions in the entire U.S. Military. These soldiers must endure the toughest training programs to become part of the elite special ops forces—but these men say their jobs are also the most rewarding.

There are three kinds of operators on the Special Tactics teams: Combat Controller, Pararescueman, and Special Ops Weatherman. In order to be a part of these teams, you must first:

- volunteer your time and efforts

- be a U.S. citizen

- be a male (based on current Department of Defense policies)

- obtain a general score of at least 43 on the Armed Services Vocational Aptitude Battery Test (the ASVAB)
- be a proficient swimmer
- be a high school graduate or have a GED
- be able to obtain a SECRET security clearance
- successfully complete the PAST (see below)
- pass an initial flying class III physical qualification of aircrew, parachute, and maritime diving duty

PHYSICAL ABILITY AND STAMINA TEST (PAST)

The PAST requirements are designed to test for a minimum fitness level for entry into the training pipeline. Candidates should continue cross-training throughout their application and the recruiting process, to exceed these minimums in order to enhance their chances of success.

- 500-meter swim (non-stop) in 15 minutes or less using any freestyle or side stroke (no fins)
- calisthenics: Candidates must exercise for full time limit or to muscle failure.
- 6 chin ups in one minute
- 50 sit-ups in two minutes
- 42 push-ups in two minutes
- 1/5 mile run (non-stop) in 11 minutes 30 seconds.

In addition, these are the basic physical requirements to apply to Special Ops:

- eyesight requirements
  - Must be at least 20/70 or better in both eyes and both correctable to 20/20 with glasses.
  - Must have normal color vision.
  - waiver possibilities: If one eye is 20/70 or better and the other no worse than 20/200, or if both eyes are no worse than 20/100.

  Note: PRK and LASIK surgery is approved by the Air Force. Applicant must wait one year after procedure; pre and post conditions must be met. LASIK is not approved for military freefall.

- flight physical
- In addition to passing a Flying Class III, you must meet age requirements:
  - Must join Air Force before 28th birthday. If person has any military time, it is subtracted from his

UNDERSTAND THE FULL MEANING

The **ASVAB**, the Armed Forces Vocational Aptitude Battery, is the entrance test to enlist in the US Military. You cannot enlist without taking it.

Cross-training refers to training in different ways to improve your overall performance.

Calisthenics are a form of exercise performed without weights or equipment to increase body strength and flexibility using body weight as resistance.

PRK and **LASIK** are ways to surgically correct vision problems so the patient no longer has to wear glasses or contacts to have 20/20 vision.

actual age, and if the result is less than 28, he can still join. For example, if the person is 31, but had four years of active duty: subtract 4 from 31 = 27.

- height: minimum height 4'10"; maximum is 6'8".
- weight: Must be in compliance with Air Force standards table. However, maximum weight for jump school is 250 pounds.

U.S. AIR FORCE SPECIAL OPERATIONS SCHOOL

The Special Operations School is the next step to becoming one of the military's most specialized soldiers.

The U.S. Air Force Special Operations School is a primary support unit of the Air Force Special Operations Command. The school directly supports the Joint Special Operations University at Hurlburt Field, Florida. It prepares special operations Airmen to successfully plan, organize, and exe-

The Motto found on the Air Force Special Operations School Crest is the Latin phrase meaning "Knowledge is strength."

Air Force Basic Training

Regardless of which branch of the Air Force you are join-ing—active duty, Air Force Reserves, or the Air National Guard, all new recruits go through the same basic train-ing at Lackland Air Force Base in San Antonio, Texas. Training lasts eight and a half weeks to turn civilians into Air Force members. Here are some recommended work-outs to prepare your mind and body for basic training. Complete the following routine 3-5 days a week, begin-ning 14 weeks prior to entering AFBMT (Air Force Basic Military Training):

- 5-minute stretch/warm-up
- 2-minute sit-up/push-up intervals
- 3-minute jog
- 17-minute run
- 3-5 minute walk
- 2-minute stretch

cute global special operations by providing indoctrination and education. The Special Operations School turns already skilled Airmen into special operators.

The final fitness test is done during the end of the seventh week of training. Air Force officials highly recommend you be able to meet these minimum fitness standards when you arrive at basic training. These minimums are not mandatory, but if you can achieve them before arriving, it will make your life much easier. Remember, these numbers are not **graduation standards**, which are much more restrictive, but the minimum recommendations for when you first arrive.

- 2-mile run: 19:16
- 1.5-mile run: 13:45
- push-ups: 34 per minute
- sit-ups: 38 per minute

It's not easy to get into the Special Forces—and once you do, life in the Air Force isn't easy. Instead, it's challenging, demanding everything you've got.

According to Susan Marquis, author of *Unconventional Warfare*,

Special operators fight a different kind of war. A war that often involves more training of other forces than fighting. A war that frequently requires observation rather than attack. A war that pits a handful of special operators against large conventional forces. A war that is most likely to take place during "peacetime," before and after military conflict, in an attempt to prevent crises or put things back together if war is unavoidable.

UNDERSTAND THE FULL MEANING

In order to graduate from Air Force Basic Military Training, you must pass minimum physical fitness standards known as **graduation standards**.

FIND OUT MORE ON THE INTERNET

Air Force www.airforce.com

Army Recruiting www.goarmy.com

Department of Defense www.defense.gov

Marine Corps www.marines.com

Navy www.navy.com

U.S. Naval Academy www.usna.edu

West Point www.usma.edu

The websites listed on this page were active at the time of publication. The publisher is not responsible for websites that have changed their address or discontinued operation since the date of publication. The publisher will review and update the websites upon each reprint.

FURTHER READING

Call, Steve. *Danger Close: Tactical Air Controllers in Afghanistan and Iraq*. College Station, Texas: TAMU Press, 2010.

Carney, John T. and Benjamin F. Schemmer. *No Room for Error: The Story Behind the USAF Special Tactics Unit*. New York: Presidio Press, 2002.

David, Jack. *Air Force Air Commandos.* Minneapolis, Minn.: Bellwether Media, 2009.

Hirsh, Michael. *None Braver: U.S. Air Force Pararescuemen in the War on Terrorism*. New York: New American Library, 2003.

Nicolls, Boone. *Airman's Guide, 7th Edition*. Mechanicsburg, Penn.: Stackpole Books, 2007.

Pushies, Fred J. *U.S. Air Force Special Ops*. Minneapolis, Minn.: Zenith Press, 2007.

Sandler, Michael. *Pararescuemen in Action*. New York: Bearport, 2008.

BIBLIOGRAPHY

Brook, Tom Vanden. "Spy planes see role in Afghan war expand," www.airforcetimes.com/news/2010/04/gns_airforce_afghan_drones_042610/ (28 April 2010).

U.S. Air Force. "Air Force medics evacuating critically ill from Haiti," www.af.mil/news/story.asp?id=123187539 (26 April 2010).

U.S. Air Force. "Air Force scientists test, develop bio jet fuels," www.af.mil/news/story.asp?id=123197415 (3 May 2010).

U.S. Air Force. "Air Force weather personnel keep Army flying," www.afweather.af.mil/news/story.asp?id=123198836 (26 April 2010).

U.S. Air Force. "Airman helps battle virus in Philippines," www.af.mil/news/story.asp?id=123191549 (26 April 2010).

U.S. Air Force. "Airmen contribute humanitarian aid to Afghan people," www.af.mil/news/story.asp?id=123200414 (26 April 2010).

U.S. Air Force. "Combat controllers bring order during chaotic times," www.af.mil/news/story.asp?id=123194016 (21 April 2010).

U.S. Air Force. "Fact Sheets—Special Topics" www.af.mil/information/factsheets/index.asp (21 April 2010).

U.S. Air Force. "Join Special Tactics," www.afsoc.af.mil/specialtactics/ (19 April 2010).

U.S. Air Force. "Learn About the Air Force," www.airforce.com/learn-about (19 April 2010).

U.S. Air Force. "Radar bound for Bagram will help pilots avoid birds," www.af.mil/news/story.asp?id=123197594 (3 May 2010).

U.S. Air Force. "Security forces help promote Iraqi community policing," www.af.mil/news/story.asp?id=123199984 (28 April 2010).

INDEX

ABOUT THE AUTHOR

Gabrielle Vanderhoof is a former competitive figure skater. She now works in publishing and public relations. This is her first time writing for Mason Crest.

ABOUT THE CONSULTANT

Colonel John Carney, Jr. is USAF-Retired, President and the CEO of the Special Operations Warrior Foundation.

PICTURE CREDITS

United States Air Force: pp. 11, 15, 17, 18, 22, 28, 36, 49, 52, 58
    Capt. Genieve David: pg. 41
    Chief Master Sgt. Gary Emery: pg. 45
    James Steele: pg. 8
    Julie Ray: pg. 26
    Master Sgt. Trish Bunting: pg. 46
    Paul Holcomb: pg. 54
    Robbin Cresswell: pg. 17

Senior Airman Joshua T. Jasper: pg. 29
Senior Master Sgt. Joy Josephson: pg. 50
Staff Sgt. Desiree N. Palacios: pg. 38
Staff Sgt. Jeff Lowry: pg. 44
Staff Sgt. Richard Williams: pg. 43
Tech. Sgt. Matthew Loy: pg. 15

To the best knowledge of the publisher, all images not specifically credited are in the public domain. If any image has been inadvertently uncredited, please notify Harding House Publishing Service, 220 Front Street, Vestal, New York 13850, so that credit can be given in future printings.